HUSTLE FORWARD, NOT BACKWARD

Charles Malone
Hustle Forward, Not Backward

Published by Spines
ISBN: 979-8-89383-455-0

HUSTLE FORWARD, NOT BACKWARD

MAMA, I MADE IT

CHARLES MALONE

CONTENTS

ROOTS IN LAGRANGE

In the heart of Lagrange, Georgia, amidst the humid Southern air and the vibrant energy of the neighborhood, Charles Malone came into the world. Born to a family entrenched in the struggles of urban life, his story unfolds against the backdrop of a community teetering between hope and hardship. Charles' childhood was shaped by the streets of Lagrange, where survival often meant navigating through the complexities of poverty and crime. Raised in a household where the shadows of financial strain loomed large, he learned resilience from his mother, who toiled tirelessly, juggling two jobs to keep the family afloat. His father's frequent brushes with the law cast a long shadow over the family, leaving Charles to grapple with the absence of a consistent paternal figure. Yet amidst the adversity, there were glimmers of light.

Charles found solace and strength in the bonds of family, leaning on his uncles for guidance and support. Their presence provided a stabilizing force in a tumultuous environment, offering him a glimpse of what it meant to weather life's storms with unwavering loyalty and love. As the oldest sibling among four, Charles assumed a mantle of responsibility from an early age, shouldering the weight of expectations while striving to carve out a path of his own. Alongside his siblings, he navigated the challenges of inner-city life, finding camaraderie and companionship in the company of his peers. Together, they formed a tight-knit group known as the DeGroat Street Boys, their bond forged through shared experiences and a mutual determination to rise above their circumstances. In the alleyways and side streets of Lagrange, Charles' journey began—a narrative woven from the threads of struggle and resilience, love and loss. His roots ran deep in the soil of his hometown, shaping the contours of a life that would unfold across a hundred chapters, each page bearing witness to the indomitable spirit of a young man determined to defy the odds.

THE WEIGHT OF RESPONSIBILITY

At the tender age of sixteen, Charles found himself thrust into the daunting role of fatherhood, a responsibility that would shape the trajectory of his life in ways he could never have imagined. Welcoming his firstborn son into the world amid the chaos of street life, he grappled with the weight of newfound obligations, navigating the delicate balance between his duties as a provider and the allure of the streets.

As the demands of fatherhood collided with the harsh realities of survival, Charles found himself drawn deeper into the shadowy underworld of Lagrange. Fueled by a potent mix of ambition and necessity, he took his first steps into the realm of street dealing, determined to carve out a future for his growing family amidst the unforgiving streets.

With each passing year, the stakes grew higher as Charles welcomed five daughters into the world, each birth marking a poignant reminder of the fragile threads that bound his burgeoning family together. Amidst the chaos of street corners and late-night deals, he found solace in the laughter and innocence of his children, their presence a beacon of hope amidst the darkness that threatened to consume him.

Yet, for all his efforts to shield his loved ones from the harsh realities of his chosen path, the specter of danger loomed ever closer, casting a shadow of uncertainty over their lives. As Charles juggled the demands of fatherhood with the risks inherent in his illicit trade, he found himself walking a tightrope stretched taut between the promise of prosperity and the specter of ruin.

In the eyes of his children, he glimpsed the reflection of his own hopes and dreams, a testament to the enduring power of love amidst the chaos of the streets. Each day brought fresh challenges and heartaches, but through it all, Charles remained steadfast in his commitment to providing for his family, a beacon of strength in a world fraught with peril.

THE CODE OF THE STREETS

In the gritty alleyways and dimly lit corners of Lagrange, Charles and his crew lived by a code as old as the streets themselves — a code forged in the crucible of survival, where loyalty was currency and silence was sacred. In a world where trust was a rare commodity, they found solace in the unspoken bond that bound them together, a brotherhood forged in the fires of adversity.

For Charles and his cohorts, the streets were more than just a battleground for turf and territory — they were a stage upon which they danced the delicate dance of survival, navigating the perilous currents of crime and consequence with a finesse born of necessity. From petty hustles to high-stakes deals, they seized every opportunity to carve out a niche in the unforgiving landscape of urban life, their wits sharpened by the constant threat of betrayal and retribution.

In the hazy glow of neon lights and the cacophony of bustling streets, Charles learned the art of the hustle from those who had mastered it before him, drawing upon their wisdom and experience to navigate the treacherous waters of the underground economy. Under the tutelage of his younger uncle, he honed his skills as a hustler, discovering new avenues of opportunity and exploiting them with ruthless efficiency.

Yet amidst the chaos and uncertainty of street life, one rule remained sacrosanct: the code of silence. In a world where betrayal carried a death sentence, Charles and his comrades adhered to a strict code of loyalty, refusing to betray one another to the authorities. Snitches were dealt with swiftly and mercilessly, their fate a grim reminder of the consequences of treachery in a world where trust was a rare and precious commodity.

As they navigated the perilous currents of street life, Charles and his crew earned a reputation as the ultimate hustlers, their ingenuity and resourcefulness unmatched in the eyes of their peers. From corner boys to kingpins, they rose through the ranks of the underworld with a swagger born of their confidence in each other and their unwavering belief in the code that bound them together.

In the crucible of the streets, Charles forged bonds that would endure a lifetime, his journey marked by the highs and lows of life on the edge. Together, they navigated the treacherous waters of the urban jungle, their footsteps echoing through the alleys and avenues of Lagrange as they pursued their dreams with a tenacity born of desperation and defiance.

4

WESTWARD BOUND

As the years rolled by and the weight of the streets grew heavier upon his shoulders, Charles found himself yearning for a fresh start—a chance to leave behind the struggles of Lagrange and forge a new path in the sun-soaked streets of California. With a heart heavy with memories and a spirit buoyed by hope, he bid farewell to the only life he had ever known and set his sights on the promise of the West.

In the sprawling metropolis of California, Charles found a canvas upon which to paint the dreams that had long eluded him—a land of opportunity where the hustle took on new forms and the possibilities seemed endless. With a hunger born of desperation and a determination forged in the crucible of the streets, he set out to carve out a niche for himself in this brave new world, armed with nothing but his wits and a steely resolve.

FROM STONES TO DIAMONDS

In the shimmering glow of California's sun-kissed beaches, Charles discovered a treasure trove of opportunities waiting to be seized. Drawing upon the skills he had honed on the streets of Lagrange, he delved into the world of legal hustles, seeking out new avenues of income with a fervor bordering on obsession.

With a keen eye for opportunity and a knack for turning raw materials into profit, Charles found himself drawn to the world of jewelry making. Armed with nothing but a handful of stones and a burning desire to succeed, he set about transforming his passion into profit, crafting exquisite pieces that caught the eye of discerning buyers from across the globe.

From the dusty mines of Africa to the bustling markets of India, Charles traversed the globe in search of the perfect stones, his quest for perfection driving him ever onward in his relentless pursuit of success. With each new gem he unearthed, he felt a sense of exhilaration coursing through his veins—a thrill that surpassed even the greatest highs of his days on the streets.

THE RISE OF A DIAMOND KING

As word of Charles' craftsmanship spread far and wide, he found himself catapulted into the upper echelons of the jewelry world. His creations were coveted by the rich and famous alike. From Hollywood starlets to titans of industry, his client list read like a who's who of the elite. Each piece he crafted was a testament to his unparalleled skill and artistry.

Yet amidst the glitz and glamour of his newfound success, Charles remained true to his roots. He never forgot the struggles that had shaped him into the man he had become. With each new commission he undertook, he remembered the faces of his friends and family back in Lagrange. Their unwavering faith in him served as a constant source of inspiration.

THE ART OF THE DEAL

As Charles's reputation as a master craftsman grew, so too did his appetite for success. With a hunger born of ambition and a drive tempered by experience, he delved into the world of high-stakes deals, seeking out opportunities to leverage his skills and connections for maximum profit.

From negotiating with suppliers to brokering deals with high-profile clients, Charles honed his skills as a dealmaker. His sharp wit and shrewd business acumen earned him a reputation as a force to be reckoned with in the cutthroat world of commerce. With each successful transaction, he felt a sense of satisfaction wash over him—a feeling that transcended the mere accumulation of wealth and spoke to the depths of his entrepreneurial spirit.

THE POWER OF CONNECTIONS

In the sprawling metropolis of California, Charles discovered the true power of connections—a web of relationships that stretched from the glittering halls of Hollywood to the bustling streets of downtown. With a charisma that drew people to him like moths to a flame, he cultivated a network of allies and associates who would prove invaluable in his quest for success.

From influential socialites to powerful brokers, Charles forged bonds that would shape the course of his career. Each connection opened doors that had long remained closed to him. With each new acquaintance he made, he felt a sense of empowerment coursing through him —a realization that in the world of business, it was not just what you knew, but who you knew that truly mattered.

THE PURSUIT OF EXCELLENCE

Driven by a relentless desire to push the boundaries of his craft, Charles immersed himself in the pursuit of excellence. He sought out new challenges and opportunities to expand his repertoire. From experimenting with new techniques to collaborating with other artisans, he embraced every opportunity to grow and evolve as an artist. His quest for perfection drove him ever onward in his relentless pursuit of greatness.

With each new creation he brought to life, Charles felt a sense of fulfillment that transcended mere material wealth—a feeling that spoke to the very core of his being and affirmed his place in the world as a true master of his craft. From humble beginnings in the streets of Lagrange to the pinnacle of success in California, his journey was a testament to the power of passion, perseverance, and the unwavering belief in oneself.

INNOVATING THE INDUSTRY

As Charles continued to make waves in the world of jewelry making, he sought to revolutionize the industry with his innovative approach to design and craftsmanship. Drawing inspiration from his surroundings and his own experiences, he pushed the boundaries of traditional techniques, experimenting with new materials and styles to create pieces that were as unique as they were breathtaking.

From sleek, modern designs to intricate, vintage-inspired creations, Charles' work captured the imagination of collectors and connoisseurs alike, each piece a testament to his boundless creativity and unparalleled skill. With each new collection he unveiled, he reaffirmed his status as a visionary artist and a trailblazer in the world of jewelry design.

11

GIVING BACK

Despite his meteoric rise to success, Charles never forgot the struggles that had shaped him into the man he had become. With a heart as generous as it was ambitious, he made it his mission to give back to the community that had supported him through thick and thin, using his newfound wealth and influence to make a positive impact in the lives of others.

From sponsoring local charities to mentoring aspiring artists, Charles poured his time and resources into initiatives aimed at uplifting those in need and empowering the next generation of entrepreneurs. Through his philanthropic efforts, he sought to honor the lessons he had learned on the streets of Lagrange and pay tribute to the family and friends who had stood by him every step of the way.

THE LEGACY CONTINUES

As the years rolled by and Charles' legacy continued to grow, he looked to the future with a sense of pride and satisfaction, knowing that he had left an indelible mark on the world around him. From the streets of Lagrange to the bustling metropolis of California, his journey had been one of triumph over adversity, of resilience in the face of hardship, and of unwavering belief in the power of the human spirit.

Though his days as a street hustler were long behind him, Charles never forgot the lessons he had learned on the streets—the value of hard work, the importance of loyalty, and the resilience of the human spirit. Through his artistry and his generosity, he sought to inspire others to reach for their dreams and never lose sight of the potential that lay within them.

THE RHYTHM OF VENICE BEACH

As the sun rose over the horizon, casting its golden rays upon the sandy shores of Venice Beach, Charles emerged from the bustling streets of California to the tranquil embrace of the ocean breeze. With a backpack full of faceted stones and a heart full of dreams, he embarked on his daily pilgrimage to the iconic boardwalk, where the rhythm of life unfolded in a kaleidoscope of color and sound.

From the moment he set foot on the sun-drenched promenade, Charles felt a sense of belonging wash over him—a feeling that transcended mere geography and spoke to the very essence of his soul. Amidst the throngs of tourists and locals alike, he found solace in the simple act of setting up his makeshift stall and laying out his wares for all to see.

THE ART OF THE SALE

With a smile as bright as the California sun and a charm that was as infectious as it was genuine, Charles set about plying his trade with the finesse of a seasoned showman. Drawing upon his natural charisma and his innate ability to connect with people from all walks of life, he captivated passersby with tales of the stones' origins and the mystical properties they possessed.

With each sale he made, Charles felt a sense of satisfaction that transcended mere monetary gain—a feeling that spoke to the joy of sharing something beautiful and unique with others. Whether it was a shimmering amethyst or a fiery opal, he took pride in knowing that he had brightened someone's day and left a lasting impression on their hearts.

FINDING BEAUTY IN THE EVERYDAY

As Charles spent his days on the sun-kissed shores of Venice Beach, he found himself drawn to the simple beauty of the world around him—a beauty that revealed itself in the laughter of children playing in the surf, the gentle caress of the ocean breeze, and the kaleidoscope of colors that danced across the horizon at sunset.

In the midst of life's hustle and bustle, he discovered a sense of peace and tranquility that he had never known before—a peace that came from being fully present in the moment and embracing the beauty of the everyday. Whether he was watching the waves crash against the shore or sharing stories with fellow vendors, he savored each moment as if it were a precious gem, knowing that life's true treasures could be found in the simple pleasures that surrounded him.

BUILDING CONNECTIONS

As Charles became a familiar presence on the boardwalk, he forged connections with the eclectic array of vendors and performers who called Venice Beach home. From the talented musicians who serenaded passersby with soulful melodies, to the quirky street artists who adorned the walls with vibrant murals, he found himself immersed in a community as colorful and diverse as the stones he sold.

With each passing day, Charles felt a sense of kinship with his fellow vendors, their shared experiences binding them together in a tapestry of friendship and camaraderie. Whether they were swapping stories over cups of coffee or lending a helping hand during busy periods, he cherished the bonds he had formed with those who shared his passion for the vibrant tapestry of life at Venice Beach.

EMBRACING THE UNEXPECTED

As Charles navigated the ebb and flow of life on the boardwalk, he learned to embrace the unexpected with open arms, finding beauty in the serendipitous moments that unfolded around him. Whether it was a chance encounter with a kindred spirit or a sudden burst of inspiration that sparked his creativity, he welcomed each new experience as a gift to be treasured and savored.

In the vibrant tapestry of Venice Beach, Charles discovered a sense of freedom and spontaneity that breathed new life into his soul, reminding him of the infinite possibilities that lay just beyond the horizon. Whether he was exploring hidden coves along the shoreline or watching the sunset from the pier, he reveled in the sense of wonder and awe that permeated every corner of this magical place.

1 8

THE END OF AN ERA

As the years passed and the sands of time shifted beneath his feet, Charles found himself reflecting on the journey that had brought him to this moment—the highs and lows, the triumphs and tribulations, the laughter and tears that had shaped his path. With each passing day, he felt a sense of gratitude wash over him, knowing that Venice Beach would always hold a special place in his heart as a sanctuary of peace and beauty amidst the chaos of the world.

But as the saying goes, all good things must come to an end, and so it was with Charles' time at Venice Beach. Though he would carry the memories of this place with him wherever he went, he knew that it was time to bid farewell to the sun-kissed shores and embark on a new chapter of his journey—one filled with new adventures, new challenges, and new opportunities waiting to be seized.

NORTHERN LIGHTS

With the sun setting on his time at Venice Beach, Charles set his sights on a new horizon, bidding farewell to the golden shores of Southern California and venturing northward to the rugged landscapes of Northern California. Drawn by the promise of new opportunities and fresh beginnings, he embraced the unknown with a sense of excitement and anticipation, eager to carve out a new path in the world of music.

THE BEAT GOES ON

As Charles settled into his new surroundings, he immersed himself in the vibrant music scene of Northern California, where the beat of the drum and the rhythm of the bass reverberated through the streets like a heartbeat. With a passion for music that burned as brightly as the California sun, he dove headfirst into the world of production and rap, channeling his experiences and emotions into the music that flowed from his soul.

FROM TRUNK TO STOREFRONT

Armed with nothing but a dream and a drive to succeed, Charles took to the streets once again, this time as a purveyor of music. From the trunk of his car, he sold mixtapes filled with his own original beats and rhymes, hustling day and night to build a following and make a name for himself in the fiercely competitive world of hip-hop. But Charles didn't stop there. With the confidence born of his independent success, he took a bold step forward and approached a local music store, pitching his CDs for sale on their shelves. To his delight, they agreed, and soon his music was reaching a wider audience than ever before, cementing his status as a rising star on the West Coast music scene.

INDEPENDENT SPIRIT

As Charles' buzz continued to grow, he remained true to his independent roots, eschewing the trappings of major labels in favor of creative freedom and artistic integrity. With each new release, he poured his heart and soul into his music, unafraid to tackle the hard truths and raw emotions that lay at the heart of his artistry. In an industry dominated by big names and bigger egos, Charles stood apart as a beacon of authenticity and originality, his music resonating with audiences far and wide. From the gritty streets of Oakland to the glitzy clubs of San Francisco, his independent spirit shone bright, inspiring others to follow their dreams and never compromise their vision for the sake of fame or fortune.

RISE TO PROMINENCE

With each beat, each lyric, and each performance, Charles' star continued to rise, shining bright in the constellation of Northern California's music scene. His unique blend of raw talent and streetwise authenticity captivated audiences and critics alike, earning him a reputation as one of the most exciting voices in hip-hop.

COLLABORATIONS AND CONNECTIONS

As Charles' reputation grew, so too did his network of collaborators and connections. From local legends to up-and-coming artists, he forged alliances that would shape the course of his career, collaborating on tracks that pushed the boundaries of genre and style. With each new collaboration, he expanded his artistic horizons and reached new audiences, cementing his status as a force to be reckoned with in the world of music.

2 5

THE GRIND NEVER STOPS

Despite his growing success, Charles remained as hungry as ever, never content to rest on his laurels or settle for mediocrity. From the recording studio to the stage, he poured every ounce of his passion and energy into his craft, pushing himself to new heights of creativity and expression with each passing day.

OVERCOMING ADVERSITY

But Charles' journey was not without its challenges. Alongside the highs came the inevitable lows—financial struggles, creative blocks, and personal setbacks that threatened to derail his dreams. Yet through it all, he persevered, drawing strength from the love and support of his family, friends, and fans, and emerging stronger and more resilient than ever before.

27

A BEACON OF HOPE

In a world fraught with uncertainty and turmoil, Charles' music served as a beacon of hope and inspiration, shining light into the darkest corners of society and giving voice to those who had been silenced by oppression and injustice. From the streets of Oakland to the halls of power in Sacramento, his lyrics spoke truth to power, challenging the status quo and advocating for change.

BREAKING BARRIERS

As Charles' music resonated with audiences across California and beyond, he found himself breaking down barriers and defying expectations at every turn. His unapologetic lyrics and fearless authenticity challenged the norms of the hip-hop industry, carving out a space for artists from all walks of life to tell their stories and be heard.

TOURING THE COAST

With his growing popularity came the opportunity to take his music on the road, embarking on a series of tours that took him from the sun-drenched beaches of Southern California to the rugged coastlines of the Pacific Northwest. With each performance, he brought his electrifying energy and magnetic stage presence to audiences far and wide, leaving a lasting impression wherever he went.

A VOICE FOR THE VOICELESS

Inspired by his own experiences growing up in the streets of Lagrange, Charles used his platform to give voice to the marginalized and the oppressed, shining a light on the social injustices that plagued his community and advocating for change. Through his music and his activism, he became a powerful force for social justice, rallying his fans to join him in the fight for a better world.

THE POWER OF COMMUNITY

Throughout his journey, Charles never lost sight of the importance of community—both in his music and in his life. From organizing charity events to supporting local businesses, he remained deeply rooted in the communities that had shaped him, giving back in any way he could and using his influence for the greater good.

LOOKING TO THE FUTURE

As Charles reflected on the path he had traveled and the obstacles he had overcome, he felt a sense of pride and gratitude for all that he had achieved. But he also knew that his journey was far from over, and that the best was yet to come. With his eyes set firmly on the future, he continued to push the boundaries of his artistry and embrace new challenges with the same passion and determination that had propelled him this far.

RETURN TO THE CITY OF ANGELS

With dreams of securing a record deal and taking his music to new heights, Charles made the decision to return to the city where it all began—Los Angeles County. Back in the heart of the sprawling metropolis, he felt a renewed sense of purpose and determination, ready to tackle the challenges that lay ahead with a steely resolve and unwavering commitment to his craft.

NAVIGATING THE INDUSTRY JUNGLE

As Charles dove headfirst into the cutthroat world of the Southern California music scene, he quickly realized that he would need to hustle harder than ever before to stand out amidst the sea of talent vying for attention. From open mics to industry showcases, he seized every opportunity to showcase his skills and make connections with key players in the industry, determined to leave a lasting impression on anyone who crossed his path.

SACRIFICES AND STRUGGLES

But with increased competition came increased pressure, and Charles soon found himself grappling with the harsh realities of the music industry. Late nights in the studio, grueling rehearsals, and endless networking events took their toll on his physical and mental well-being, forcing him to make sacrifices and tough choices in pursuit of his dreams.

RISING ABOVE THE NOISE

Despite the challenges and setbacks he faced, Charles refused to be deterred, drawing strength from the adversity he encountered and using it as fuel to propel him forward. With each rejection, he grew more determined to prove his critics wrong and show the world what he was truly capable of achieving.

THE HEART OF A HUSTLER

In the unforgiving landscape of the Southern California music scene, Charles' hustle became his greatest asset, propelling him to new heights of success and recognition. From street performances to guerrilla marketing tactics, he left no stone unturned in his quest for greatness, leveraging every opportunity to elevate his career and make his mark on the industry.

CREATIVE EVOLUTION

As Charles immersed himself in the vibrant music scene of Southern California, he underwent a process of creative evolution, exploring new sounds, styles, and influences that pushed the boundaries of his artistry. From experimenting with different beats and rhythms to collaborating with diverse artists from across the region, he embraced every opportunity to grow and evolve as a musician, constantly pushing himself to new heights of creativity and innovation.

BUILDING ALLIANCES

Recognizing the power of collaboration in an industry driven by connections, Charles forged alliances with fellow artists, producers, and industry insiders, pooling their talents and resources to amplify their collective impact. Together, they formed a tight-knit community of creatives united by a shared vision and a common goal—to elevate each other's careers and leave a lasting legacy on the Southern California music scene.

SEIZING OPPORTUNITIES

In the fast-paced world of the music industry, opportunities came and went in the blink of an eye, and Charles knew that he had to seize every chance that came his way with unwavering determination and tenacity. From high-profile showcases to chance encounters with industry heavyweights, he leveraged every opportunity to showcase his talent and make a lasting impression on those who held the keys to his success.

STAYING TRUE TO HIMSELF

Amidst the glitz and glamour of the Southern California music scene, Charles remained grounded in his roots, staying true to himself and his unique artistic vision. Refusing to compromise his integrity for the sake of fame or fortune, he remained steadfast in his commitment to authenticity, pouring his heart and soul into every lyric, every beat, and every performance.

THE LONG ROAD AHEAD

As Charles continued to navigate the twists and turns of the Southern California music scene, he knew that the road ahead would be long and fraught with challenges. But armed with his unwavering determination, his unshakable faith in himself, and his relentless hustle, he was ready to face whatever obstacles lay in his path and emerge victorious on the other side.

FINDING RESILIENCE

In the face of setbacks and disappointments, Charles found resilience in the depths of his soul, refusing to let adversity define him or dictate the course of his journey. With each obstacle he encountered, he grew stronger and more determined, channeling his setbacks into fuel for his relentless pursuit of success.

PUSHING BOUNDARIES

As Charles honed his craft and refined his sound, he pushed the boundaries of his artistry, daring to explore new genres, experiment with unconventional melodies, and challenge the status quo. With each daring leap into uncharted territory, he defied expectations and blazed a trail of his own, leaving an indelible mark on the landscape of Southern California music.

EMBRACING VERSATILITY

Recognizing the value of versatility in an ever-changing industry, Charles embraced a diverse range of musical styles and influences, from soulful R&B ballads to hard-hitting hip-hop anthems. With each new venture outside his comfort zone, he expanded his artistic horizons and reached new audiences, cementing his reputation as a dynamic and multifaceted artist.

LEARNING FROM FAILURE

In the pursuit of greatness, failure was inevitable, but Charles refused to let it define him. Instead, he embraced each setback as an opportunity for growth and learning, extracting valuable lessons from every misstep and using them to fuel his evolution as an artist and entrepreneur.

CULTIVATING DISCIPLINE

In a world filled with distractions and temptations, Charles cultivated discipline with unwavering resolve, committing himself to a rigorous regimen of practice, self-improvement, and personal development. With each passing day, he honed his skills, sharpened his focus, and fortified his determination to achieve his goals no matter the cost.

NAVIGATING RELATIONSHIPS

As Charles' star continued to rise, he found himself navigating the complexities of personal and professional relationships in the spotlight. From managing collaborations and creative partnerships to balancing the demands of fame and family, he learned to navigate the delicate dance of interpersonal dynamics with grace and integrity.

EMBRACING SUCCESS

With each milestone reached and each accolade earned, Charles embraced the success that came his way with humility and gratitude, never losing sight of the journey that had brought him to this moment. Whether performing on stage to adoring fans or receiving industry recognition for his achievements, he remained grounded in the knowledge that true success was measured not by fame or fortune, but by the impact he had on others.

THE LEGACY LIVES ON

As Charles reflected on the chapters of his life that had brought him to this point, he knew that his journey was far from over. With his eyes set firmly on the future, he continued to write new chapters in the story of his life, each one a testament to the power of passion, perseverance, and the unwavering belief in oneself.

INSPIRING OTHERS

In the midst of his own success, Charles never lost sight of the importance of paying it forward and inspiring the next generation of artists to follow their dreams. Whether mentoring aspiring musicians, giving back to his community, or using his platform to advocate for positive change, he remained committed to leaving a legacy that extended far beyond his own achievements.

THE JOURNEY CONTINUES

As Charles looked ahead to the road that stretched before him, he knew that the journey ahead would be filled with twists and turns, triumphs and tribulations. But with each step forward, he remained steadfast in his belief that anything was possible with hard work, dedication, and a relentless commitment to chasing his dreams.

53

EMBRACING THE UNKNOWN

With the future stretching out before him like an open road, Charles embraced the unknown with open arms, knowing that the greatest adventures were yet to come. With each new challenge and opportunity that awaited him, he welcomed the uncertainty of what lay ahead, knowing that it was only through embracing the unknown that he would truly discover his full potential.

FINDING BALANCE

In the midst of his relentless pursuit of success, Charles sought to find balance in his life, carving out time for self-care, reflection, and personal fulfillment amidst the demands of his career. Whether spending time with loved ones, indulging in his hobbies, or simply taking a moment to pause and appreciate the beauty of the world around him, he recognized the importance of nourishing his mind, body, and soul.

CELEBRATING MILESTONES

As Charles reached new milestones in his career, he took time to celebrate the achievements and victories that marked his journey. Whether it was releasing a new album, selling out a concert venue, or receiving critical acclaim for his work, he relished each moment of success and allowed himself to bask in the glow of his hard-earned accomplishments.

GRATITUDE AND HUMILITY

Amidst the whirlwind of fame and fortune, Charles remained grounded in gratitude and humility, never losing sight of the people and experiences that had shaped him into the person he had become. From his humble beginnings in Lagrange to the bright lights of Southern California, he recognized that every step of his journey had been guided by the love and support of those who believed in him.

EMBRACING CHANGE

As the music industry continued to evolve and change, Charles embraced the shifting tides with adaptability and resilience, always staying one step ahead of the curve. Whether exploring new avenues of distribution, embracing emerging technologies, or experimenting with innovative marketing strategies, he remained at the forefront of the industry, constantly reinventing himself and his sound to stay relevant in an ever-changing landscape.

LEAVING A MARK

With each song he wrote, each stage he graced, and each life he touched, Charles left a mark on the world that would endure long after he was gone. Whether inspiring others through his music, advocating for social change, or simply spreading joy and positivity wherever he went, he knew that his legacy would live on in the hearts and minds of those who had been touched by his artistry and his spirit.

THE POWER OF DREAMS

In the end, Charles' journey was a testament to the power of dreams—the belief that with enough passion, perseverance, and determination, anything was possible. From the streets of Lagrange to the bright lights of Southern California, he had dared to dream big and chase those dreams with unwavering conviction, leaving behind a legacy that would inspire generations to come.

THE ENDLESS SYMPHONY

As Charles reached the final chapter of his story, he knew that the music would never truly end. For in the hearts and minds of those who had been touched by his artistry, his spirit would live on forever; an endless symphony of hope, inspiration, and the boundless power of the human spirit.

HOMECOMING

After years of chasing his dreams on the West Coast, Charles felt the pull of home tugging at his heartstrings, prompting him to return to Columbus, Georgia. Back in the town where it all began, he found solace in the familiar sights and sounds of his childhood, reconnecting with old friends and family members who welcomed him with open arms.

NEW BEGINNINGS

With a desire to build a stable future for himself and his loved ones, Charles sought out opportunities for employment in his hometown, eventually landing a job at Enterprise car rental. Embracing his role with enthusiasm and dedication, he threw himself into his work, eager to prove himself in this new chapter of his life.

THE ART OF CUSTOMER SERVICE

At Enterprise, Charles discovered a newfound passion for customer service, delighting in the opportunity to connect with people from all walks of life and provide them with exceptional experiences. Whether helping a family find the perfect rental car for their vacation or assisting a business traveler with their transportation needs, he took pride in delivering top-notch service with a smile.

CLIMBING THE CORPORATE LADDER

Driven by ambition and a thirst for success, Charles set his sights on climbing the corporate ladder at Enterprise, seizing every opportunity for growth and advancement that came his way. Through hard work, dedication, and a knack for leadership, he steadily rose through the ranks, earning promotions and accolades for his outstanding performance.

A DECADE OF DEDICATION

As the years flew by, Charles dedicated himself wholeheartedly to his career at Enterprise, celebrating a decade of service with the company—a milestone that filled him with pride and gratitude. Through the ups and downs, the challenges and triumphs, he remained steadfast in his commitment to excellence, earning the respect and admiration of his colleagues and superiors alike.

RETIREMENT REFLECTIONS

After ten years of loyal service, Charles made the bittersweet decision to retire from Enterprise, bidding farewell to a chapter of his life that had been filled with growth, learning, and cherished memories. As he reflected on his time with the company, he felt a sense of gratitude for the opportunities he had been given and the friendships he had forged along the way.

A NEW CHAPTER BEGINS

With retirement came the dawn of a new chapter in Charles' life—one filled with endless possibilities and exciting opportunities. Freed from the constraints of the corporate world, he set his sights on pursuing his passions and exploring new avenues of self-expression and creativity.

DISCOVERING CONTENT CREATION

Inspired by his love of storytelling and his desire to share his experiences with the world, Charles stumbled upon the world of content creation—a platform that allowed him to showcase his creativity and connect with like-minded individuals from around the globe. Through blogging, vlogging, and social media, he found a new outlet for his passion and a way to make money doing what he loved.

THE POWER OF PASSION

As Charles delved deeper into the world of content creation, he discovered the power of passion in driving success and fulfillment. Whether producing videos about his travels, sharing tips on car maintenance, or offering insights into his life journey, he poured his heart and soul into his work, knowing that authenticity was the key to connecting with his audience.

EMBRACING ENTREPRENEURSHIP

With his newfound success as a content creator, Charles embraced the entrepreneurial spirit, turning his passion into a profitable business venture. From sponsored content deals to merchandise sales, he found innovative ways to monetize his platform and generate income while doing what he loved.

BUILDING A BRAND

As Charles' online presence grew, so too did his brand, evolving into a recognized name in the world of content creation. Through strategic branding and marketing efforts, he cultivated a loyal following of fans and supporters who eagerly awaited his next post or video, eager to join him on his journey of self-discovery and adventure.

SHARING WISDOM

With years of life experience under his belt, Charles embraced his role as a mentor and guide, sharing wisdom and insights gleaned from his own journey with his audience. Whether offering career advice, personal development tips, or reflections on life's ups and downs, he sought to inspire and uplift others on their own paths to success and fulfillment.

FINDING BALANCE

As Charles juggled the demands of content creation with the joys of retirement, he prioritized finding balance in his life, carving out time for relaxation, recreation, and quality time with loved ones. By nurturing his mind, body, and soul, he ensured that he remained grounded and centered amidst the whirlwind of his newfound success.

GIVING BACK

Never one to forget his roots, Charles remained committed to giving back to his community, using his platform to raise awareness for causes close to his heart and support those in need. Whether fundraising for local charities, volunteering his time, or lending his voice to advocacy efforts, he sought to make a positive impact on the world around him.

THE JOURNEY CONTINUES

As Charles looked ahead to the future, he knew that the journey was far from over. With each new day came new opportunities for growth, learning, and self-discovery, and he approached each challenge with a spirit of optimism and adventure. Whether exploring new creative projects, embarking on exciting adventures, or simply savoring the moments of joy and connection that life had to offer, he embraced the journey with open arms and an open heart.

CREATIVE EXPANSION

As Charles delved deeper into the world of content creation, he found himself drawn to new and exciting avenues of creative expression. From podcasting to photography, he embraced a diverse range of mediums, pushing the boundaries of his artistry and exploring new ways to connect with his audience.

PERSONAL GROWTH

With each new project and collaboration, Charles experienced profound personal growth, challenging himself to step outside his comfort zone and embrace the unknown. Through self-reflection and introspection, he gained valuable insights into his own strengths and weaknesses, learning to embrace his vulnerabilities and harness them as sources of strength.

ENTREPRENEURIAL VENTURES

Fuelled by his entrepreneurial spirit, Charles embarked on a series of new ventures, from launching his own merchandise line to partnering with brands on innovative marketing campaigns. With each new business endeavor, he honed his skills as a savvy entrepreneur, learning to navigate the complexities of the digital marketplace with confidence and finesse.

CONNECTING WITH THE COMMUNITY

As his online presence continued to grow, Charles remained committed to fostering a sense of community and connection among his followers. Through live streams, virtual meet-ups, and interactive Q&A sessions, he engaged directly with his audience, forging meaningful connections and building a loyal fan base that spanned the globe.

EMBRACING DIVERSITY

Recognizing the importance of diversity and inclusion in the online space, Charles made a conscious effort to amplify diverse voices and perspectives within his content. Whether featuring guest creators from underrepresented backgrounds or shining a spotlight on issues of social justice and equality, he used his platform to advocate for a more inclusive and equitable online community.

MENTORSHIP AND GUIDANCE

Drawing upon his own experiences as a content creator, Charles took on the role of mentor and guide to aspiring creators looking to break into the industry. Through coaching sessions, workshops, and online tutorials, he shared his expertise and insights, empowering others to pursue their passions and build successful careers in content creation.

COLLABORATION AND PARTNERSHIP

In the spirit of collaboration, Charles sought out opportunities to partner with fellow creators and brands on joint projects and initiatives. Whether co-hosting podcasts, collaborating on video series, or launching co-branded products, he leveraged the power of collaboration to expand his reach and amplify his impact within the online community.

ADAPTABILITY IN A CHANGING LANDSCAPE

As the digital landscape continued to evolve, Charles remained adaptable and resilient, staying ahead of trends and embracing new technologies to stay relevant in an ever-changing industry. From experimenting with emerging platforms to mastering the art of algorithmic optimization, he remained agile and proactive in navigating the shifting currents of the online world.

CELEBRATING MILESTONES

With each new milestone and achievement, Charles took time to celebrate the successes and victories that marked his journey as a content creator. Whether reaching a new subscriber milestone, securing a major brand partnership, or receiving industry recognition for his work, he paused to reflect on how far he had come and express gratitude for the support of his fans and followers.

BALANCING WORK AND PLAY

Amidst the demands of content creation, Charles prioritized finding balance in his life, carving out time for rest, relaxation, and self-care. Whether taking leisurely walks in nature, indulging in creative hobbies, or spending quality time with loved ones, he recognized the importance of nurturing his well-being and replenishing his creative energy.

EMBRACING AUTHENTICITY

At the core of his content creation journey, Charles remained committed to authenticity and transparency, sharing his true self with his audience and inviting them to join him on his journey. Whether sharing candid reflections on his life experiences or documenting the highs and lows of his creative process, he remained true to his values and beliefs, inspiring others to do the same.

GRATITUDE AND REFLECTION

As Charles looked back on his journey as a content creator, he felt an overwhelming sense of gratitude for the opportunities and experiences that had shaped him along the way. From the early days of hustling mixtapes out of his trunk to the present moment of creative fulfillment and financial success, he recognized the blessings that had been bestowed upon him and vowed to pay it forward by continuing to inspire and uplift others through his work.

LEGACY AND IMPACT

With each piece of content he created and shared with the world, Charles left a lasting legacy that extended far beyond the confines of the digital realm. Whether inspiring others to pursue their passions, advocating for social change, or simply spreading joy and positivity, he made a meaningful impact on the lives of those who had been touched by his work, leaving behind a legacy of creativity, compassion, and connection.

LOOKING AHEAD

As he stood on the threshold of a new chapter in his life and career, Charles felt a sense of excitement and anticipation for the adventures that lay ahead. With each sunrise came new opportunities for growth, learning, and self-discovery, and he embraced the journey with open arms and an open heart, knowing that the best was yet to come.

THE NEVER-ENDING STORY

For Charles, the journey of content creation was a never-ending story—a tale of creativity, connection, and endless possibility. As long as there were stories to tell, ideas to explore, and hearts to touch, he would continue to share his voice with the world, weaving a tapestry of inspiration and imagination that would endure for generations to come.

THE HUSTLER'S SPIRIT

Despite achieving success and recognition as a content creator, Charles never lost sight of the hustler's spirit that had propelled him to greatness. With a tireless work ethic and an insatiable drive for success, he approached every project with the same hunger and determination that had fueled his rise from the streets of Lagrange to the digital stage of content creation.

CREATIVE ENTREPRENEURSHIP

As a content creator, Charles embraced the principles of creative entrepreneurship, constantly seeking out new opportunities to monetize his passion and maximize his earning potential. From sponsored content deals to affiliate marketing partnerships, he leveraged his platform to generate multiple streams of income, ensuring that his hustle translated into tangible financial success.

DIVERSIFYING REVENUE STREAMS

Recognizing the importance of diversification in an ever-changing digital landscape, Charles sought to expand his revenue streams beyond traditional advertising and sponsorship deals. From launching his own line of merchandise to offering premium content subscriptions, he explored innovative ways to monetize his audience and future-proof his income against market fluctuations.

STRATEGIC BRAND PARTNERSHIPS

Through strategic brand partnerships, Charles forged mutually beneficial alliances with companies and organizations that aligned with his values and resonated with his audience. By collaborating with brands that shared his commitment to authenticity and quality, he was able to monetize his content while maintaining the trust and loyalty of his fan base.

HUSTLING SMARTER, NOT HARDER

As Charles' career as a content creator flourished, he learned the importance of hustling smarter, not harder. By leveraging automation tools, outsourcing non-essential tasks, and prioritizing high-impact activities, he was able to maximize his productivity and efficiency, allowing him to achieve more in less time without sacrificing quality or creativity.

EMBRACING CHALLENGES

In the face of challenges and obstacles, Charles embraced the opportunity to innovate and adapt, turning adversity into opportunity and setbacks into stepping stones for growth. Whether navigating changes in platform algorithms, overcoming creative blocks, or weathering fluctuations in audience engagement, he remained resilient and resourceful in the pursuit of his goals.

MENTORSHIP AND GUIDANCE

Drawing upon his own experiences as a hustler and content creator, Charles sought to mentor and guide aspiring entrepreneurs and creators looking to follow in his footsteps. Through coaching programs, mastermind groups, and online courses, he shared his knowledge and expertise, empowering others to unleash their full potential and achieve success on their own terms.

PAYING IT FORWARD

With success came a sense of responsibility for Charles, who remained committed to paying it forward and giving back to those who had supported him along the way. Whether through charitable donations, community outreach initiatives, or mentorship programs, he sought to uplift and empower others, ensuring that his hustle made a positive impact on the world around him.

NEVER SETTLING

Despite his achievements, Charles never rested on his laurels or became complacent in his pursuit of success. With each milestone reached and each goal accomplished, he set his sights even higher, constantly challenging himself to reach new heights of excellence and innovation in his work as a content creator and entrepreneur.

THE LEGACY OF THE HUSTLER

As Charles reached the milestone of 100 chapters in his journey, he reflected on the legacy of the hustler that had guided him throughout his life and career. From his humble beginnings in Lagrange to his current status as a respected content creator and entrepreneur, he had never wavered in his commitment to hard work, determination, and relentless pursuit of his dreams.

Charles' journey as a hustler has been filled with challenges, triumphs, and endless opportunities for growth. As he continues to hustle his way to success in the ever-changing landscape of content creation, one thing remains certain: the spirit of the hustler will always burn bright within him, driving him forward on his journey to greatness.